Contents

CW01202475

Icons used in this book

🔵 This 'pointer' icon marks the brief introduction that sets the piece of writing in context and provides useful background information.

🔵 This 'be safe' icon marks important information relating to the use of the text – including personal safety.

You will find it helpful to have a dictionary to refer to when you are using this book.

The rooks' parliament

The origins of the collective term 'a parliament of rooks' lie in the fact that rooks are most commonly seen in flocks, and will sometimes form large groups in which one bird will 'speak' at length. Although young rooks look similar to crows, the adult rook has a longer beak and black feathers, while the crow's feathers are black with a green and purple sheen.

Rooks are not stunted crows. They are black,
Hunch quietly on fields in plough.
I woke as a child to their raw
Kind cawing. The shooters then came
5 Claimed they were pests. We lifted them back,
Their eyes' light a chilling blue flame.

The marksmen were wrong. Rooks eat pests.
The blunt-headed crows in their pairs
Rip road-kills; while rooks' beaks, slim, bare,
10 Prod every clod in their slow crowd.
Rookeries crown rough roadside trees
With clambered sticks, thriving and loud.

A strange story hovers like birds,
That their field circlings form grave
15 Assemblies where wisdom is made
To rule their land well, with a caw.
We cannot. Dare they? I am glad
We do not shoot rooks any more.

Alison Brackenbury

1 a) Why do you think the poet starts with a statement of what rooks **are not** like before saying what they **are** like?

_____

1 mark

   b) What does the statement tell us of her expectations of people's knowledge and opinions?

_____

_____

1 mark

2 What adjective in the first verse attributes a human emotion to the rooks?

_____

1 mark

3 A metaphor is a figure of speech in which a word or phrase that usually describes one thing is used to describe another.

   a) What metaphor does the poet use in the opening verse?

_____

1 mark

   b) What is it that the poet describes using this metaphor?

_____

1 mark

4 Which phrase tells us that rooks build their nests high above ground?

_____

1 mark

5 We talk about a 'flock of birds', but rooks have their own collective noun: 'a parliament of rooks'. Look in a dictionary to find the origin and meaning of the word 'parliament'.

   a) It comes from _____

       meaning _____ .

1 mark

   b) Why do you think the poet chose the phrase as this poem's title?

_____

_____

1 mark

6 What is the meaning of 'grave' in the third verse (line 14)?

_____

1 mark

7 **In your own words**, explain why the poet is 'glad we do not shoot rooks any more'. Include one example of how they benefit our environment.

_____

_____

1 mark

_____

page 5
total out of 10

Tudor wedding

 The fictional character Eva De Puebla, who is from Spain, is an interpreter and lady-in-waiting to the real-life Catherine of Aragon, who is also Spanish. Here Eva describes Catherine's wedding to King Henry VII's 14-year-old son Arthur. Arthur was the older brother of Henry ('Harry'), who later became Henry VIII.

14th November 1501, London, England

The wedding. And what a day it's been! A whirlwind of colour and pageantry and feasting and wine – heavens, how these English drink! They are said to be the most truculent, law-resistant people in Europe, united among themselves only when fighting a common enemy, but their appetite for revelry is almost
5   frightening. The King had caused the fountains to flow with burgundy wine after the marriage was celebrated, and the crowds were gulping it from their cupped hands, yelling and cheering, surging to and fro, careless of those who had fallen insensible and were being trampled over.

Catherine remained serene throughout it all. She looked lovely – as fresh and
10 young as a girl making her First Communion – in her gown of white satin and with her long hair held by a circlet of gold and pearls. Those of us who had sat for so long stitching pierced seed pearls on to her veil with fine gold thread were rewarded when we saw her standing in that shimmer of delicate brightness. I wish Mama could have seen it – she would have been so proud.

15 Arthur, too, looked beautiful in his white clothes, and in the cathedral the pair of them stood out like two white swans against the deep, rich scarlet of the draperies and the massed gorgeousness of the courtiers. Margaret was gowned in cloth of gold as befits the future Queen of Scotland, and little Mary wore a dress of crimson velvet. Harry was in a richly embroidered tunic and a fur-
20 trimmed cloak, and when the ceremony ended, it was he who escorted Catherine down the aisle to the waiting people massed outside. His face was proud and unsmiling, and I had the feeling that he was impatient with his youth, cursing it for casting him as the second son and not the elder.

We came in grand procession to Baynard's Castle, and feasted throughout
25 the afternoon and evening. Gold platters gleamed in the light of hundreds of candles, and servants came in with course after course of soups and pies and roast meats (venison, rabbit, goose, swan and suckling pig) and then great cheeses and sweets (jellies and trifles and brandy-soaked cakes) – all served with an abundance of wine.

From *My Tudor Queen – The Diary of Eva De Puebla, London 1501–1513*
Alison Prince

1 Where did the bride come from?

_____ 1 mark

2 Give the meaning of the following words:

a) truculent: _____ 1 mark

b) serene: _____ 1 mark

3 A simile is a way of comparing two things that are not usually seen as similar – and it often uses the word 'like'. What simile in this text describes the wedding couple?

_____ 1 mark

4 Why might Harry have wished he were the older brother on the day described here?

_____

_____ 1 mark

5 **Three** different shades of red are mentioned describing different elements of the celebrations, from the wine to the fabrics. Name the **three** shades.

_____

_____

_____ 3 marks

6 From how far through the book do you think this extract is taken? Explain your answer.

_____

_____ 1 mark

7 Underline a statement of opinion in the following quotation from the text.

'Margaret was gowned in cloth of gold as befits the future Queen of Scotland, and little Mary wore a dress of crimson velvet.' 1 mark

Review

_____

_____

_____

_____

The way through the woods

Rudyard Kipling was the British writer and poet who wrote *The Jungle Book* and the *Just So Stories*, which are still popular with children today. He wrote 'The way through the woods' for a young girl called Christabel, who was a friend of his daughter. When he asked Christabel if she had enjoyed a recent holiday in the New Forest, she told Kipling that she had been frightened of ghosts there. Her remark inspired him to write this poem.

They shut the road through the woods
Seventy years ago.
Weather and rain have undone it again,
And now you would never know
5   There was once a road through the woods
Before they planted the trees.
It is underneath the coppice and heath
And the thin anemones.
Only the keeper sees
10   That, where the ring-dove broods,
And the badgers roll at ease,
There was once a road through the woods.

Yet, if you enter the woods
Of a summer evening late,
15   When the night air cools on the trout-ringed pools
Where the otter whistles his mate,
(They fear not men in the woods,
Because they see so few),
You will hear the beat of a horse's feet,
20   And the swish of a skirt in the dew,
Steadily cantering through
The misty solitudes,
As though they perfectly knew
The old lost road through the woods.
25   But there is no road through the woods.

Rudyard Kipling (1865–1936)

1 Name the flowers that grow where the road once ran through the woods.

_____   1 mark

2 What clues are there that few people walk in the woods?

_____

_____   1 mark

3 What clues are there that the horse and rider were not really there?

_____

_____   1 mark

4 Apart from the horse's hooves and the swish of the skirt, what other sound can be heard in the woods?

_____   1 mark

5 Explain the meaning of 'solitudes'.

_____   1 mark

6 What causes rings to appear on the surface of the pools?

_____   1 mark

7 If you were reciting the poem, where might you
a) change tempo?
b) change volume?
Explain **how** and **why**.

a) _____

_____

_____

b) _____

_____

_____   4 marks

page 9
total out of 10

Chocolate

 Roald Dahl is best known for his children's novels — including *Matilda* (which features in **Key Stage 2 Comprehension Book 3**) and *The Enormous Crocodile* (**First Comprehension Book 1**). This extract is taken from *Boy*, in which Roald Dahl describes his time at Repton School. It explains the origin of his lifelong love of chocolate — and the source of inspiration for one of his books.

Every now and again, a plain grey cardboard box was dished out to each boy in our House, and this, believe it or not, was a present from the great chocolate manufacturers, Cadbury. Inside the box there were twelve bars of chocolate, all of different shapes, all with different fillings and all with numbers from one to
5   twelve stamped on the chocolate underneath. Eleven of these bars were new inventions from the factory. The twelfth was the 'control' bar, one that we all knew well, usually a Cadbury's Coffee Cream bar. Also in the box was a sheet of paper with the numbers one to twelve on it as well as two blank columns, one for giving marks to each chocolate from nought to ten, and the other for comments.

10   All we were required to do in return for this splendid gift was to taste very carefully each bar of chocolate, give it marks and make an intelligent comment on why we liked it or disliked it.

It was a clever stunt. Cadbury's were using some of the greatest chocolate-bar experts in the world to test out their new inventions. We were of a sensible age,
15   between thirteen and eighteen, and we knew intimately every chocolate bar in existence, from the Milk Flake to the Lemon Marshmallow. Quite obviously our opinions on anything new would be valuable. All of us entered into this game with great gusto, sitting in our studies and nibbling each bar with the air of connoisseurs, giving our marks and making our comments. 'Too subtle for the
20   common palate,' was one note that I remember writing down.

For me, the importance of all this was that I began to realize that the large chocolate companies actually did possess inventing rooms and they took their inventing very seriously. I used to picture a long white room like a laboratory with pots of chocolate and fudge and all sorts of other delicious fillings bubbling away
25   on the stoves, while men and women in white coats moved between the bubbling pots, tasting and mixing and concocting their wonderful new inventions. I used to imagine myself working in one of these labs and suddenly I would come up with something so absolutely unbearably delicious that I would grab it in my hand and go rushing out of the lab and along the corridor and right into the office of the
30   great Mr Cadbury himself. "I've got it, sir!" I would shout, putting the chocolate in front of him. "It's fantastic! It's fabulous! It's marvellous! It's irresistible!"

From *Boy, Tales of Childhood*
Roald Dahl (1916–90)

1 Roald Dahl is well known as a **fiction** writer. What makes this extract **non-fiction?**

_____ 1 mark

2 The memories described here inspired Roald Dahl to write one of his novels. Which novel was this?

_____ 1 mark

3 Why do you think the samples of new chocolate bars were stamped with numbers and not names?

_____

_____ 1 mark

4 a) Which chocolate bar was usually used as a 'control bar'?

_____ 1 mark

b) What would be its purpose?

_____ 1 mark

5 **In your own words**, explain the meaning of the phrase 'entered into this game with great gusto' (line 17).

_____ 1 mark

6 a) Why did Dahl consider the boys of Repton School to be 'experts' in the consumption and enjoyment of chocolate?

_____ 1 mark

b) Which other word does Dahl use that means 'knowledgeable experts'?

_____ 1 mark

7 What do you think Dahl meant by 'too subtle for the common palate' (line 19)?

_____ 1 mark

8 In Dahl's imagination he invents the perfect chocolate bar. Of the four enthusiastic adjectives he uses to describe it, which one suggests that people won't be able to stop themselves from eating it?

_____ 1 mark

Two owls

Owls have rounded heads and forward-facing eyes, giving them features that some recognise as a 'face'. Perhaps this is one reason why they are often written about. Found all over the world, most owls are active during the night and at dawn and dusk.

The owl

Downhill I came, hungry, and yet not starved;
Cold, yet had heat within me that was proof
Against the North wind; tired, yet so that rest
Had seemed the sweetest thing under a roof.

5 Then at the inn I had food, fire, and rest,
Knowing how hungry, cold, and tired was I.
All of the night was quite barred out except
An owl's cry, a most melancholy cry

Shaken out long and clear upon the hill,
10 No merry note, nor cause of merriment,
But one telling me plain what I escaped
And others could not, that night, as in I went.

And salted was my food, and my repose,
Salted and sobered, too, by the bird's voice
15 Speaking for all who lay under the stars,
Soldiers and poor, unable to rejoice.

Edward Thomas (1878–1917)

Owl

Why does night rest its gourd in my breast?
Why does the moon puff out my feathers?
Why do mice twinkle like stars?
Why does the darkness hoot in my ears?
5 Why does a hollow tree seem like heaven?
I am so bespectacled with questions,
The poor fools call it wisdom.

John Agard

1 Both these poems are written in (ring **one**):   the first person   the third person.

1 mark

2 a) At the opening of the first poem, what three feelings could have made the speaker feel

dejected? _____

1 mark

    b) Why does he not feel downhearted? _____

_____

1 mark

3 What similarities are there between Thomas's 'inn' and Agard's 'hollow tree'? _____

_____

2 marks

4 What does 'no merry note' and 'nor cause of merriment' tell us about both the owl and the

speaker, in the first poem? _____

1 mark

5 a) Which adjective describing the owl's cry also sums up the speaker's feelings on hearing the

bird? _____

1 mark

    b) What does the word mean? _____

1 mark

6 What thoughts preoccupy the traveller's mind at the end of Thomas's poem? _____

_____

_____

1 mark

7 In Agard's poem, who is asking the questions? _____

1 mark

8 A question to which no answer is expected is described as (ring **one**):

methodical   analytical   rhetorical   impractical   artificial.

1 mark

9 From the second poem, quote an example of

1 mark

    a) a simile _____

    b) a metaphor _____

1 mark

10 Do you think it is a warm or a cold night in the second poem? Explain your answer. _____

_____

1 mark

11 Give one example of how Thomas's poem is more traditional than Agard's in style and form.

_____

1 mark

12 What common human belief about owls is challenged in Agard's poem? _____

_____

1 mark

page 13
total out of 16

Mammoth find

Complete baby turns up in Siberia

 The word 'mammoth' comes from the Russian word *mamont*. This is the name given to a type of elephant, sometimes with long curved tusks and long hair, which lived many thousands of years ago. 'Mammoth' is also used to mean gigantic (or 'as large as a mammoth').

Its tail is lopsided. Close up, it looks suspiciously like a small, and unremarkable, Asian elephant.

5 But scientists were yesterday hailing the sensational discovery of a perfectly preserved baby woolly mammoth, which died around 10 000 years ago and was found in the frozen tundra of northern Russia. Experts said 10 the six-month-old female calf was a rare complete specimen. The animal's trunk and eyes are intact. It even has fur.

A reindeer herder, Yuri Khudi, 15 stumbled across the carcass in May near the Yuribei river in Russia's Yamal-Nenents autonomous district, in a virtually inaccessible part of north-western Siberia.

20 Extinct woolly mammoths – and giant tusks – have turned up in Siberia for centuries. But it is unusual for a complete example to be recovered. The last major find was in 1997 25 when a family in the neighbouring Taymyr Peninsula came across a tusk attached to what turned out to be a 20 380-year-old mammoth carcass.

The latest 130cm tall, 50kg Siberian 30 specimen appears to have died just as the species was heading for extinction during the last Ice Age. It is being sent to Japan for further tests.

"The mammoth has no defects except 35 that its tail was a bit off," Alexei Tikhonov, one of a group of international experts who examined the mammoth last week in the Arctic town of Salekhard, told BBC Online. 40 He added: "In terms of its state of preservation, this is the world's most valuable discovery."

Global warming has made it easier for woolly mammoth hunters to hack 45 the animal out of Russia's thawing permafrost. An entire mammoth industry has sprung up around the far eastern frontier town of Yakutsk.

Many examples are simply sold on 50 the black market – and can be seen in Russian souvenir shops, next to unhappy-looking stuffed brown bears.

Mammoths first appeared around 48 million years ago. Most of them 55 died out 12 000 years ago at the end of the Pleistocene era.

Luke Harding
Wednesday 11 July 2007,
Guardian, Moscow

Glossary

autonomous having the right to govern itself
carcass dead body
permafrost soil that is permanently frozen
Pleistocene the period of history when the last great Ice Age occurred

1 a) In the opening paragraph, to what does the pronoun 'it' refer?

_____   1 mark

b) Why did the journalist choose to use this pronoun before saying what he is writing about?

_____

_____   1 mark

2 What is 'tundra'?

_____

_____   1 mark

3 In which part of Russia was the mammoth found?

_____   1 mark

4 The remains of other woolly mammoths have been found before. What aspects of **this** find are particularly exciting?

_____

_____   2 marks

5 What gender was the woolly mammoth?

_____   1 mark

6 What expression does the journalist use early in the report, based on Tikhonov's observation that 'its tail was a bit off'?

_____   1 mark

7 How do unscrupulous people try to make money out of smaller finds like this?

_____   1 mark

8 What is a 'black market'?

_____

_____   1 mark

9 When did the woolly mammoth species become extinct?

_____   1 mark

10 What sentence in this report might make readers hope for further information about this find in due course?

1 mark

_____

Poems that entertain

 There are many kinds of poetry – and this page gives you the opportunity to think about what they may have in common and how they are different from each other. Most poems are pieces of imaginative writing, set out in lines and offering us one possible way of understanding the world. Here they also provide us with entertainment – and amusement.

Crocodile's tale

The last man who mistook me for a log
Lost half-a-foot and can no longer jog.

John Agard

There was an old lady

There was an old lady whose folly
Induced her to sit in a holly;
    Whereupon by a thorn,
    Her dress being torn,
5 She quickly became melancholy.

Edward Lear (1812–88)

Magic

A web
captures the storm:
glass beads, safe in fine net,
gather sunlight as they sway in
5 high winds.

Judith Nicholls

Haiku

Half-time score: Nil Nil
Ravenous, the goal mouth gapes
Longing for a ball.

Peggy Poole

The amorous teacher's sonnet to his love

Each morning I teach in a daze until
the bell that lets me hurry down and queue
with pounding heart to wait for you to fill
my eyes with beauty and my plate with stew.
5 Dear dinner lady, apple of my eye,
I long to shout I love you through the noise
and take your hand across the shepherd's pie
despite the squealing girls or snickering boys.
O let us flee together and start up
10 a little cafe somewhere in the Lakes
and serve day trippers tea in china cups
and buttered scones on pretty patterned plates.

Alas for dreams so rudely bust in two –
some clumsy child's spilt custard on my shoe.

Dave Calder

1. These poems represent five different forms. Fill in the gaps to complete the table below.

Title of poem and poet	Poetic form	Brief description of form
'The amorous teacher's sonnet to his love', Dave Calder	sonnet	● three sets of four lines rhyming ABAB, CDCD, EFEF and a closing couplet rhyming GG ● line rhythm identical throughout
a) _____ _____	b) _____ _____	● five-line verse (usually comical) rhyming AABBC ● strong metre ● lines 3 and 4 shorter
c) _____ _____	couplet	d) _____ _____
'Magic', Judith Nicholls	cinquain	● five-line verse with syllable count for successive lines: 2-4-6-8-2
e) _____ _____	haiku	f) _____ _____

6 marks

2. In the poem 'Magic' what are the metaphorical 'glass beads'?

_____

1 mark

3. Which **two** poems are written in the first person?

_____

2 marks

4. Which poem most clearly personifies an inanimate object? Explain how this is done.

_____

_____

2 marks

5. In 'Crocodile's tale', how did the man lose half his foot?

_____

1 mark

6. Which **two** poems do **not** use rhyme?

_____

2 marks

7. In 'The amorous teacher's sonnet to his love', line 6, the poet does not use conventional speech punctuation. Rewrite the line using speech marks and a comma correctly.

_____

1 mark

8. What is the meaning of the phrase 'apple of my eye' in the amorous teacher's sonnet?

_____

1 mark

Child employment

 Some young teenagers have paid work to do at weekends or during the school holidays. To make sure that they are kept safe and to ensure that work does not disrupt their education, there are special laws related to child employment. Some of these are summarised below.

Compulsory school age

Children are of compulsory school age up to the last Friday in June in the academic year in which they reach the Mandatory School Leaving Age (MSLA) and the child can apply for their National Insurance Number and may work full time.

5 The youngest age your child can work part-time is 13 years old, with the exception of children involved in television, theatre, modelling or similar activities.

If a child is offered work in these areas, they will need to get a performance licence. Performance licences are issued by the local authority. Before granting a licence the local authority will liaise with the headteacher of the child's school to ensure that 10 the child's education will not suffer should that licence be granted.

Chaperoning

A child taking part in a performance – which can include TV, film, theatre, sporting activities or modelling – will require chaperoning. Chaperones are licensed by the local authority.

15 Children may not work:

- without an employment permit issued by the education department of the local council
- in any industrial setting e.g. factory, industrial site etc.
- during school hours
- 20 before 7.00 am or after 7.00 pm
- for more than one hour before school
- for more than four hours without taking a break of at least one hour
- in any occupations prohibited by local by-laws or other legislation e.g. pubs, betting shops
- 25 in any work that may be harmful to their health, well-being or education
- without having a two-week break from any work during the school holidays in each calendar year

Term time

During term time children may work a maximum of 30 12 hours per week, of which:

- a maximum of two hours on school days and
- a maximum of five hours on Saturdays for 13 to 14 year olds, or eight hours for children aged 15 35 and over

This information was correct at the time of publication, but you should not use it as a source of reference without checking that it is still current.

1 The academic year begins on 1 September and ends on 31 August. Jack reached the MSLA on 31 July. Indira reached the MSLA just over a month later, on 1 September.

a) When can Jack leave school?

_____ 1 mark

b) When can Indira leave school?

_____ 1 mark

2 a) What does MSLA stand for?

_____ 1 mark

b) What does 'mandatory' mean?

_____ 1 mark

3 Each person who starts working full-time has a unique identification number related to employment. What name is given to that number?

_____ 1 mark

4 Lily and Eve are 12-year-old schoolgirls who want to work part-time after school. Lily wants to work in a local shop and Eve wants to model for an advertising agency. Which, if either, of the girls is allowed to do their chosen job? Explain the conditions.

_____

_____ 2 marks

5 During term-time how long per week are 16-year-olds allowed by law to work?

_____ 1 mark

6 Anil, aged 15, wanted to work after school, from 4 p.m. to 6 p.m., in a biscuit factory. The factory owner said she could not employ him. Why not?

_____ 1 mark

7 For what sort of work would a child need a licence? What sort of licence would be required?

_____ 2 marks

8 What is a chaperone and for what sort of work would a child need one?

_____

_____ 2 marks

9 As a child working part-time, where would you apply for an employment permit?

_____ 1 mark

page 19
total out of 14

To the cuckoo

 The poet William Wordsworth often wrote about the beauty of nature, using language that was simple and accessible to readers of his time. Here he describes the sound of the cuckoo, which has a distinctive two-note call. Because cuckoos spend the winter in Africa, only returning to Europe in April, they are often seen as the bringers of spring.

O blithe newcomer! I have heard,
    I hear thee and rejoice.
O cuckoo! shall I call thee bird,
    Or but a wandering voice?

5 While I am lying on the grass
    Thy twofold shout I hear;
From hill to hill it seems to pass,
    At once far off and near.

Though babbling only to the vale
10   Of sunshine and of flowers,
Thou bringest unto me a tale
    Of visionary hours.

Thrice welcome, darling of the Spring!
    Even yet thou art to me
15 No bird, but an invisible thing,
    A voice, a mystery;

The same whom in my schoolboy days
    I listened to; that cry
Which made me look a thousand ways
20   In bush, and tree and sky.

To seek thee did I often rove
    Through woods and on the green;
And thou wert still a hope, a love;
    Still longed for, never seen.

25 And I can listen to thee yet;
    Can lie upon the plain
And listen, till I do beget
    That golden time again.

O blessèd bird! the earth we pace
30   Again appears to be
An unsubstantial, fairy place;
    That is fit home for thee!

William Wordsworth (1770–1850)

1. In this poem, Wordsworth describes the cuckoo using the two-word name 'Blithe newcomer'. What four-word name does he use to describe the same bird?

_____

1 mark

2. Give **one** of the phrases that describe the cuckoo's voice.

_____

1 mark

3. Why does the speaker describe the cuckoo as 'no bird, but an invisible thing'?

_____

_____

1 mark

4. If 'twice' means two times, what does 'thrice' mean?

_____

1 mark

5. Is the speaker hearing the cuckoo for the first time? Explain how you know.

_____

_____

1 mark

6. Hearing the cuckoo has two main effects on the speaker (tick **two**):

   a) it reminds him of his childhood

   b) it leads him up the garden path

   c) it makes the earth seem slightly unreal

   d) it encourages him to fall in love.

2 marks

7. Which word does the poet mark with an accent, which tells us to read it as two syllables?

_____

1 mark

Review

_____

_____

_____

_____

page 21
total out of 8

The magic of shells

Shells are made by tiny animals called molluscs, which have soft bodies and no bones. The shells are formed on the outside of their bodies so that they can stay safe inside. Many of the shells we find on the beach are empty, because the molluscs have died; a few may still have the molluscs inside them.

Walking along a shell-dappled beach, it's easy to see why some of our ancestors thought that shells had dropped from the stars. Seashells are, of course, the homes of animals known as molluscs, and, usually, you will see two groups on our beaches: gastropods, which include marine snails such as limpets, periwinkles, dog whelks and
5 winkles; and bivalves – animals with two shells hinged together, such as clams, cockles, mussels and oysters.

What kind of shells you encounter depends on the beach. Sandy shorelines are more congenial to razor-shells, cockles, oysters and whelks. Limpets are a good bet on most beaches, while cockles love mud. Coastal beaches, exposed to the full brunt of
10 winter storms, are handy for mussels, which attach themselves to boulders on rocky shores and seek havens in rock pools.

Looking at all those motionless shells, you might wonder what their purpose is. Though they look inactive, a vital part of the global food chain is, imperceptibly, taking place. Top-shells are important for clearing algae off rocks, while at high
15 tide, limpets perform a similar task, walking from point to point, acting as nature's rubbish collectors. "A lot of shells are important for life on the beach," says Cat Ridout, Marine Awareness Officer for the Devon Wildlife Trust at Wembury Marine Centre. "The seaweed they eat passes energy to the creatures that eat them, such as starfish, crabs and fish." Not all seashells are herbivores, though. The cowrie eats
20 seasquirts, while the dog whelk consumes other snails, using acid on its tongue tip to drill a hole through other shells.

Conservationists are keen to strike a balance when it comes to taking away holiday souvenirs. Mankind has probably gathered seashells since the dawn of time, while excavations in South Africa have dated shells strung as beads to around 75 000 BC.
25 Many Aboriginal peoples relied on them for food, and some coastal communities in developing countries still do. Henry VIII supposedly wore a shirt bound with seashells, and shells have long been adapted as oil lamps.

"It would be silly to say, 'don't take any shells away'," said Simon Ford, the National Trust's Nature Conservation Adviser for Wessex. "But on some beaches large numbers
30 of pebbles have been removed with a significant impact on erosion. I doubt the impact would be the same on shells, but they're important for the ecology of the beach. They produce calcium when they break down and large amounts of our beaches are made from such shells." Cat suggests that taking a couple of shells home is perfectly acceptable. "In the long term, taking a lot of shells is not sustainable,"
35 she said. "But if you do take some, always make sure they are empty."

Abridged from the article of the same title by Mark Rowe
National Trust Magazine, Summer 2007

1. Long ago, where did some people think shells came from?

_____

1 mark

2. What are the **two** main groups of shelled sea-creatures?

_____

_____

2 marks

3. a) What name is given to creatures that are vegetarian and therefore eat no meat?

_____

1 mark

   b) Name **two** shellfish that **do** eat meat.

_____

_____

1 mark

4. Why does Simon Ford suggest that it would be 'silly' to say, "Don't take any shells away"?

_____

_____

1 mark

5. How does the dog whelk get inside the shells of snails it wants to eat?

_____

_____

1 mark

6. Quote **one** statement of fact and **one** statement of opinion from the final paragraph.

   Fact: _____

   Opinion: _____

2 marks

7. If you picked up some shells to take home, what would be the most important thing to check first?

_____

1 mark

8. What message, if any, does the writer want to pass on to his readers?

_____

1 mark

9. How does the last paragraph help the writer to achieve his objective?

_____

_____

1 mark

page 23
total out of 12

Our toilsome journey

The novel *Kidnapped* (first published in 1886) is a gripping adventure story containing many historical details about what it was like to be in Scotland after the important battle that took place there in 1745. The main character David Balfour, and his friend Alan Breck Stewart, survive both kidnapping and a shipwreck. In this extract, they are on a dangerous quest to obtain some money owed to Balfour by a wealthy uncle.

The mist rose and died away, and showed us that country lying as waste as the sea; only the moorfowl and the pewees crying upon it, and far over to the east, a herd of deer, moving like dots. Much of it was red with heather; much of the rest broken up with bogs and hags and peaty pools; some had been burnt black

5 in a heath fire; and in another place there was quite a forest of dead firs, standing like skeletons. A wearier-looking desert man never saw; but at least it was clear of troops, which was our point.

We went down accordingly into the waste, and began to make our toilsome and devious travel towards the eastern verge. There were the tops of mountains all round

10 (you are to remember) from whence we might be spied at any moment; so it behoved us to keep in the hollow parts of the moor, and when these turned aside from our direction to move upon its naked face with infinite care. Sometimes, for half an hour together, we must crawl from one heather bush to another, as hunters do when they are hard upon the deer. It was a clear day again, with a blazing sun; the water in the brandy

15 bottle was soon gone; and altogether, if I had guessed what it would be to crawl half the time upon my belly and to walk much of the rest stooping nearly to the knees, I should certainly have held back from such a killing enterprise.

Toiling and resting and toiling again, we wore away the morning; and about noon lay down in a thick bush of heather to sleep. Alan took the first watch; and it seemed to me

20 I had scarce closed my eyes before I was shaken up to take the second. We had no clock to go by; and Alan stuck a sprig of heath in the ground to serve instead; so that as soon as the shadow of the bush should fall so far to the east, I might know to rouse him. But I was by this time so weary that I could have slept twelve hours at a stretch; I had the taste of sleep in my throat; my joints slept even when my mind was waking; the hot

25 smell of the heather, and the drone of the wild bees, were like possets to me; and every now and again I would give a jump and find I had been dozing.

From *Kidnapped*
Robert Louis Stevenson (1850–94)

1 a) Why do the deer appear to be 'moving like dots'?

_____

1 mark

b) Why do the fir trees look 'like skeletons'?

_____

1 mark

2 Why were the travellers crawling and stooping as they moved across the moor?

_____

_____

1 mark

3 Who were the travellers keeping watch for?

_____

1 mark

4 At what time of day did they stop for a sleep? (ring **one**):

dawn   midday   sunset   midnight

1 mark

5 Which senses were stimulated to make the speaker feel sleepy when on watch? (ring **three** and quote a supporting phrase alongside each of your choices):

sight	
smell	
sound	
taste	
touch	

3 marks

6 Explain how the travellers' makeshift clock worked.

_____

_____

1 mark

7 What do you think will happen next in the story? Explain your answer.

_____

_____

1 mark

Diogenes and the Cynics

 Philosophy is the study of ideas about the human race, what it believes, and how it relates to the rest of the natural world. It is thought that philosophy began in Greece in about 600 BC. The philosopher Diogenes expressed his ideas in some unusual ways!

Diogenes slept in a barrel to show how slight and simple are the needs of mankind. This belief that we do not need money or comfortable surroundings was one of the views held by a group of philosophers known as the Cynics. The Cynics were members of a sect, founded by Antisthenes in around 400 BC, to which Diogenes belonged. The

5 word 'cynic' as it was used in Ancient Greece meant 'canine' or 'dog-like'. It seemed an appropriate name for this group because the Cynics were surly like dogs. They were proud people who didn't care what others thought or said about them. They despised luxury, desired nothing and worried little about their own welfare.

Dressed in rags, Diogenes personified frugality. Letting his beard grow long and

10 unkempt, he roamed about Athens with his barrel on his shoulder. His only other possessions were a cloak, a stick and a bread bag. Alexander the Great once visited Diogenes when he was sitting beside his barrel. "What can I do to please you?" enquired the great leader, who was curious to meet this unusual man.

"Just get out of my light – you're blocking the sun," replied the Cynic.

15 This plain and proud answer pleased the monarch so much that he went away thinking, "If I were not Alexander the Great, I would wish to be Diogenes."

The famous Cynic Diogenes was so unconcerned about what would become of him that he allowed a fellow citizen to sell him as a slave. However, Diogenes' new master, who was a Corinthian, soon discovered the intellect of this strange man and

20 entrusted to him the education of his son. Diogenes died in 323 BC, aged 96. The people of his native town, Sinope, on the Black Sea, erected statues to his memory and decorated his tomb with the marble head of a dog.

1 The following words could be used to describe Diogenes. What do they mean?

a) an intellectual:

_____

b) frugal:

_____

2 marks

2 Name **one** other adjective used in this text that could be used to describe Diogenes.

_____

1 mark

3 To what do the words 'cynic' and 'canine' both relate?

_____

1 mark

4 Who started the philosophical sect of Cynics?

_____

1 mark

5 **In your own words**, explain what Alexander the Great admired about Diogenes.

_____

_____

1 mark

6 Having bought Diogenes as a slave, what job did his Corinthian master give him?

_____

1 mark

7 Which verb does the author use that means 'asked'?

_____

1 mark

8 Write down **one** fact and **one** opinion about Diogenes from this passage.

Fact: _____

Opinion: _____

2 marks

page 27
total out of 10

Welcoming Grace

 This extract from the novel *The Woodlanders* by Thomas Hardy is about Giles Winterborne and Grace Melbury, who had grown up together in the small woodland community of Little Hintock but drift apart when Grace's father sends her away to school. On her return, Giles gives a party, which is attended by other woodlanders such as Farmer Cawtree. Giles plans to win Grace over, relying on his employee Robert Creedle to serve the meal — but not everything goes to plan.

"...There, he's calling for more plates. Lord, why can't 'em turn their plates bottom upward for pudding, as we bucks used to do in former days!"

Meanwhile in the adjoining room Giles was presiding in a half-unconscious state. He could not get over the initial failures in his scheme for advancing his suit; and hence he did not
5 know that he was eating mouthfuls of bread and nothing else, and continually snuffing the two candles next to him till he had reduced them to mere glimmers drowned in their own grease. Creedle now appeared with a specially prepared stew, which he served by elevating the little three-legged crock that contained it and tilting the contents into a platter on the table, exclaiming simultaneously, "Draw back, gentlemen and ladies, please!"

10 A splash followed. Grace gave a quick involuntary nod and blink, and put her handkerchief to her face.

"Good heavens! what did you do that for, Creedle?" said Giles sternly, jumping up.

"'Tis how I do it when they bain't here, maister," mildly expostulated Creedle, in an aside audible to all the company.

15 "Well, yes – but – " replied Giles. He went over to Grace, and hoped none of it had gone into her eye. "O no," she said. "Only a sprinkle on my face. It was nothing."

"Kiss it and make it well," gallantly observed Mr Cawtree.

Miss Melbury blushed.

The timber-merchant replied quickly, "O, it is nothing! She must bear these little mishaps."
20 But there could be discerned in his face something which said, "I ought to have foreseen all this, and kept her away."

Giles himself, since the untoward beginning of the feast, had not quite liked to see Grace present. He wished he had not asked such people as Cawtree and the hollow-turner. He had done it, in dearth of other friends, that the room might not appear empty. In his mind's
25 eye, before the event, they had been the mere background or padding of the scene; but somehow in the reality they were the most prominent personages there.

From *The Woodlanders*
Thomas Hardy (1840–1928)

1 a) The direct speech of Robert Creedle reflects his colloquial (informal) way of speaking. In the opening speech, what word would replace the word ''em' if he spoke formally?

_____

1 mark

b) Give, and explain, another colloquialism as spoken by Creedle.

_____

2 marks

2 How did Creedle plan to keep the washing-up to a minimum?

_____

_____

1 mark

3 Giles's 'scheme for advancing his suit' refers to his plans to (tick **one**):

a) ensure Grace doesn't go hungry

b) encourage Grace to mend his clothes

c) invite Grace to marry him.

1 mark

4 Name **one** of the things Giles did unknowingly that showed his anxiety.

_____

1 mark

5 What suggests that Creedle must have known his method of dishing up could splash people sitting at the table?

_____

1 mark

6 What made Miss Melbury blush?

_____

1 mark

7 What does 'dearth' (of other friends) mean?

_____

1 mark

8 Do you think Grace will be impressed by the party? Explain your answer.

_____

_____

1 mark

Scott of the Antarctic

Robert Falcon Scott (1868–1912) was born in Plymouth and on leaving school he was all set for a career at sea. By 1882 he was training to be an officer in the Royal Navy and in the years that followed he was promoted several times. In 1899 he was offered command of an expedition to the Antarctic. This was the start of Scott's passionate interest in exploring one of the coldest regions of the world.

The South Pole is the southernmost point of the Earth in an enormous freezing continent called Antarctica. It is so cold that, in places, the ice is three miles thick. Wind speeds can accelerate suddenly from quiet conditions to 40mph, making the already cold temperatures feel even colder through the wind-chill effect.

5 In the early twentieth century, British explorer Captain Robert Falcon Scott longed to be the first man to reach the South Pole. In 1912, with a small party, he set off in an attempt to fulfil his ambition. It was destined to end in disaster. When he reached the South Pole and raised the Union flag of Great Britain, Scott found the flag of Norway already flying. Norwegian explorer Roald Amundsen had got there first.

10 Heading back, conditions were dreadful, with blizzards and gale force winds. The men were exhausted. They had limited food and were suffering from scurvy, an illness caused by a lack of vitamin C in their diet. Struggling on despite frostbite and 'snow blindness', the men pulled the sledges themselves.

Two months after reaching the Pole, one of the group, Evans, died. Another, Oates, 15 unable to continue because of severe frostbite in his feet, did not want to slow his companions' progress. In a brave gesture, he left their tent, saying, "I am just going outside, and I may be some time."

Scott, the last of the remaining three to die, recorded his words in a number of letters and notes that he wrote in his log book, which was found months later, with their 20 dead bodies. When a search party found them eight months later, they were lying in their sleeping bags inside their tent, covered in snow. Tragically, they were only 11 miles short of their next food depot.

Captain Scott's letters told the world of their bravery and stoicism in the final weeks of their lives. Back in London, a huge memorial service was held in the explorers' 25 honour. This service was led by the king and took place in St Paul's Cathedral. In Scott's last letter to his wife, or 'widow', as he knew she would be when she read it, he expressed the wish that she should make their son 'interested in natural history'. He did not live to see his son grow up to become a respected and famous naturalist, ornithologist and wildlife artist – knighted Sir Peter Scott, in 1973, for his services to 30 conservation.

On page 32, you can read extracts from Captain Scott's last letter from the Antarctic.

1 Which word means 'to increase in speed'?

_____ 1 mark

2 What is the most noticeable effect of the strong winds on a visitor to the Antarctic?

_____ 1 mark

3 What was Captain Scott's ambition when he left home in 1912?

_____ 1 mark

4 a) Complete this sentence: British is to Britain as Norwegian is to ...

_____ . 1 mark

b) 'British' and 'Norwegian' are (ring **one**):

nouns   verbs   adjectives   proper nouns. 1 mark

5 Scurvy is caused by a dietary lack of what?

_____ 1 mark

6 a) What did Oates intend his companions to infer from his last words?

_____

_____ 1 mark

b) For what practical reasons did he make his 'brave gesture'?

_____

_____ 1 mark

7 The party died 'only' 11 miles from a food depot. Why was that distance too far for the men to cover at this stage in their journey?

_____

_____ 1 mark

8 If Captain Scott could have seen his son grow up, why might he have been proud of him?

_____

_____ 1 mark

Scott's last letter

'To my widow ...'

 This is an extract from the last letter that Scott wrote to his wife. Sadly, he and his four companions on the journey to the South Pole (including Titus Oates, who is mentioned in the letter) all died on their way back. Later, a memorial was put up at the point where their tent was found, with the words 'to strive, to seek, to find and not to yield'.

Dearest Darling – we are in a very tight corner and I have doubts of pulling through – In our short lunch hours I take advantage of a very small measure of warmth to write letters preparatory to a possible end – the first is naturally to you on whom my thoughts mostly dwell waking or sleeping – if anything
5 happens to me I shall like you to know how much you have meant to me and that pleasant recollections are with me as I depart. – I should like you to take what comfort you can from these facts also – I shall not have suffered any pain but leave the world fresh from harness and full of good health and vigour ...

10 We have gone down hill a good deal since I wrote the above. Poor Titus Oates has gone – he was in a bad state – the rest of us keep going and imagine we have a chance to get through but the cold weather doesn't let up at all – we are now only 20 miles from a depot but we have very little food or fuel ...

I must write a little letter for the boy if time can be found to be read when he
15 grows up ... I hope I shall be a good memory certainly the end is nothing for you to be ashamed of and I like to think that the boy will have a good start in parentage of which he may be proud. Dear it is not easy to write because of the cold – 70 degrees below zero and nothing but the shelter of our tent.

... Since writing the above we have got to within 11 miles of our depot with one
20 hot meal and two days' cold food and we should have got through but have been held for four days by a frightful storm – I think the best chance has gone.

... I have written letters on odd pages of this book – will you manage to get them sent? You see I am anxious for you and the boy's future – make the
25 boy interested in natural history if you can, it is better than games – they encourage it at some schools – I know you will keep him out in the open air – try and make him believe in a God, it is comforting ...

1 Explain what Scott means by the following phrases:

a) 'in a tight corner':

_____

b) 'doubts of pulling through':

_____

c) 'gone down hill':

_____

2 a) Which phrase means 'in readiness for'?

_____

b) What is the meaning of the word 'vigour'?

_____

3 a) Who does Scott mainly think about and dream of towards the end of his expedition?

_____

b) Which phrase means 'happy memories'?

_____

4 Was this letter written all at once or over several days? Quote from the text to support your answer.

_____

_____

5 a) What reason does Scott give for the fact that it was physically difficult to write?

_____

b) Under easier circumstances, where, in the third paragraph, might Scott have used a full-stop and a capital letter?

_____

6 As he is writing to his wife, why does Scott address his letter 'to my widow'?

_____

7 Give **one** of Scott's main wishes for his son's upbringing.

_____

page 33
total out of 12

Carried with a mighty force

Robinson Crusoe is based on the true story of Alexander Selkirk who, in 1704, ran away to sea and was eventually put ashore on an uninhabited island. The author, Daniel Defoe, added many exciting incidents to make the true story more interesting. In this extract, Crusoe is swept back and forth by the sea as he tries to reach dry land.

Nothing can describe the confusion of thought which I felt when I sank into the water; for though I swam very well, yet I could not deliver myself from the waves so as to draw breath, till that wave having driven me, or rather carried me, a vast way on towards the shore, and having spent itself, went back, and left me
5   upon the land almost dry, but half dead with the water I took in. I had so much presence of mind, as well as breath left, that seeing myself nearer the mainland than I expected, I got upon my feet, and endeavoured to make on towards the land as fast as I could before another wave should return and take me up again; but I soon found it was impossible to avoid it; for I saw the sea come after me as high as a great hill,
10   and as furious as an enemy, which I had no means or strength to contend with: my business was to hold my breath, and raise myself upon the water if I could; and so, by swimming, to preserve my breathing, and pilot myself towards the shore, if possible, my greatest concern now being that the sea, as it would carry me a great way towards the shore when it came on, might not carry me back again with it when it gave back
15   towards the sea.

The wave that came upon me again buried me at once twenty or thirty feet deep in its own body, and I could feel myself carried with a mighty force and swiftness towards the shore – a very great way; but I held my breath, and assisted myself to swim still forward with all my might. I was ready to burst with holding my breath, when, as I
20   felt myself rising up, so, to my immediate relief, I found my head and hands shoot out above the surface of the water; and though it was not two seconds of time that I could keep myself so, yet it relieved me greatly, gave me breath and new courage. I was covered again with water a good while, but not so long but I held it out; and finding the water had spent itself, and began to return, I struck forward against the return of
25   the waves, and felt ground again with my feet.

From *Robinson Crusoe*
Daniel Defoe (1660–1731)

1. The speaker's 'confusion of thought' on first sinking suggests that he was mostly feeling (ring **one**):

   embarrassed   perky   panic-stricken   emotional   discontent.

   1 mark

2. What does the speaker mean by 'could not deliver myself from the waves'?

   _____

   1 mark

3. The wave 'having spent itself' means that the wave has (ring **one**):

   used up its energy   drowned me   enjoyed itself.

   1 mark

4. **In your own words**, explain why Crusoe, having landed on dry land, couldn't prevent himself from again being washed out to sea.

   _____

   _____

   1 mark

5. What simile does the author use to describe the ferocity of the sea?

   _____

   1 mark

6. Find words in the story that have the same meaning as the following words:

   a) 'steer' or 'drive': _____

   1 mark

   b) 'tried', 'attempted': _____

   1 mark

   c) 'speed': _____

   1 mark

7. Describe what you think might happen on Robinson Crusoe's first night on the island.

   _____

   _____

   1 mark

8. This piece of prose consists of long sentences, unbroken by any shorter phrases or direct speech. How does this contribute to the effectiveness of the description and scene creation?

   _____

   _____

   1 mark

Review

_____

_____

_____

page 35
total out of 10

Victorian Christmas

This extract from the famous novel *A Christmas Carol* by Charles Dickens (published in 1843) describes nineteenth-century London in the depths of winter. Taken from the first chapter of the book, it also introduces the main character, Scrooge.

Meanwhile the fog and darkness thickened so, that people ran about with flaring links, proffering their services to go before horses in carriages, and conduct them on their way. The ancient tower of a church, whose gruff old bell was always peeping slily down at Scrooge out of a Gothic window in the wall, became invisible, and struck the hours and
5 quarters in the clouds, with tremulous vibrations afterwards as if its teeth were chattering in its frozen head up there. The cold became intense. In the main street, at the corner of the court, some labourers were repairing the gas-pipes, and had lighted a great fire in a brazier, round which a party of ragged men and boys were gathered: warming their hands and winking their eyes before the blaze in rapture. The water-plug being left in solitude,
10 its overflowings sullenly congealed, and turned to misanthropic ice. The brightness of the shops where holly sprigs and berries crackled in the lamp-heat of the windows, made pale faces ruddy as they passed. Poulterers' and grocers' trades became a splendid joke: a glorious pageant, with which it was next to impossible to believe that such dull principles as bargain and sale had anything to do. The Lord Mayor, in the stronghold of the
15 Mansion House, gave orders to his fifty cooks and butlers to keep Christmas as a Lord Mayor's household should; and even the little tailor, whom he had fined five shillings on the previous Monday for being drunk and bloodthirsty in the streets, stirred up tomorrow's pudding in his garret, while his lean wife and the baby sallied out to buy the beef.

20 Foggier yet, and colder! Piercing, searching, biting cold. If the good Saint Dunstan had but nipped the Evil Spirit's nose with a touch of such weather as that, instead of using his familiar weapons, then indeed he would have roared to lusty purpose. The owner of one scant young nose, gnawed and mumbled by the hungry cold as bones are gnawed by dogs, stooped down at Scrooge's keyhole to regale him with a Christmas carol: but at the first
25 sound of "God bless you, merry gentleman! May nothing you dismay!" Scrooge seized the ruler with such energy of action that the singer fled in terror, leaving the keyhole to the fog and even more congenial frost.

From *A Christmas Carol*
Charles Dickens (1812–70)

Glossary

congenial friendly, good natured
flaring links burning torches
garret loft or attic room
regale entertain
sallied out set out, went out
scant small, slight

1 What service were people offering to carriage drivers in the fog and darkness?

_____

1 mark

2 What was hidden from view that indicates the density and depth of the fog?

_____

1 mark

3 How is the tolling of the bell described?

_____

1 mark

4 What is the name of the container that enables a coal or charcoal fire to be lit in the street?

_____

1 mark

5 The ice is described as 'misanthropic'. What does that mean?

_____

1 mark

6 What was the general mood of people that day? Give an example to support your answer.

_____

_____

1 mark

7 What were the opening words of the Christmas carol sung at Scrooge's door?

_____

1 mark

8 What made the carol singer run away?

_____

_____

1 mark

Review

_____

_____

_____

_____

page 37
total out of 8

From father to son

This is an extract from Shakespeare's play *Hamlet*, which was written in 1603–04. Polonius – who is councillor to the court of the King of Denmark – gives advice to his hot-tempered son Laertes.

Act I, Scene iii

                  Give thy thoughts no tongue,
Nor any unproportioned thought his act.
Be thou familiar, but by no means vulgar.
Those friends thou hast, and their adoption tried,
5 Grapple them unto thy soul with hoops of steel;
But do not dull thy palm with entertainment
Of each new-hatch'd, unfledged comrade. Beware
Of entrance to a quarrel, but being in,
Bear't that the opposed may beware of thee.
10 Give every man thy ear, but few thy voice;
Take each man's censure, but reserve thy judgment.
Costly thy habit as thy purse can buy,
But not express'd in fancy; rich, not gaudy;
For the apparel oft proclaims the man,
15 And they in France of the best rank and station
Are of a most select and generous chief in that.
Neither a borrower nor a lender be;
For loan oft loses both itself and friend,
And borrowing dulls the edge of husbandry.
20 This above all: to thine own self be true,
And it must follow, as the night the day,
Thou canst not then be false to any man.
Farewell: my blessing season this in thee!

From *Hamlet*, Act I, Scene iii
William Shakespeare (1564–1616)

Glossary

apparel dress, clothing
censure criticism, disapproval, scorn
grapple fasten tightly
habit dress, clothing
unfledged untested (like a baby bird's wings)
unproportioned not carefully considered
vulgar crude, coarse, offensive

1 Complete the glossary below.

comrade: _____

1 mark

rank and station: _____

1 mark

husbandry: _____

1 mark

2 Imagine that you have a son, and you are giving him the same advice as Polonius did to his son, Laertes. In your own words, sum up the essence of his advice on the following subjects.

a) private thoughts	
b) casual friendship	
c) close friendship	
d) dealing with quarrels	
e) clothing	
f) money matters	
g) honesty	

7 marks

3 Quote one piece of advice from the original text that you would like to follow in your own life today. Explain why it is as valid now as it was over 400 years ago.

_____

_____

2 marks

_____

page 39
total out of 12

Book 4
total out of 200

Schofield&Sims

the long-established educational publisher specialising in maths, English and science

Key Stage 2 Comprehension provides a unique collection of 72 stimulating texts that appeal to both boys and girls, together with questions that build comprehension skills and widen vocabulary. Readers are also given intensive practice in observing how different kinds of writing are structured and in identifying literary devices and their effects. Comprising four one-per-child pupil books, the series is designed for children in Years 3 to 6 and is also suitable for some older pupils.

The **Key Stage 2 Comprehension** pupil books support the National Curriculum and provide a permanent record of each child's work, helping you to monitor progress.

The series provides:

- a **brief introduction** with useful background information, which sets each piece of writing in context

- passages from **classic and contemporary fiction** to broaden pupils' reading experience

- a wide selection of **poetry**, from Dylan Thomas to John Agard

- stimulating **non-fiction** extracts, with different subjects and structures

- a **range of question types**, including direct, inferential and evaluative questions.

Key Stage 2 Comprehension Book 4 is for pupils in Year 6 (ages 10–11) with broadening interests and vocabulary. Eighteen carefully selected texts reflect the range of genres recommended by the National Curriculum and questions are clearly presented on the facing page. The fourth of four **Key Stage 2 Comprehension** pupil books, this book features work by writers such as Thomas Hardy and Alison Brackenbury as well as Robert Scott's last letter to his widow and a short extract from *Hamlet*.

The separate **Teacher's Guide** contains teaching notes, sample answers and further activities for each text, allowing you to use **Key Stage 2 Comprehension** to its full potential.

The full range of books in the series is as follows.

Key Stage 2 Comprehension Book 1   ISBN 978 07217 1154 6
Key Stage 2 Comprehension Book 2   ISBN 978 07217 1155 3
Key Stage 2 Comprehension Book 3   ISBN 978 07217 1156 0
Key Stage 2 Comprehension Book 4   ISBN 978 07217 1157 7
Key Stage 2 Comprehension Teacher's Guide   ISBN 978 07217 1158 4

First Comprehension is available for younger children.

ISBN 978-07217-1157-7

9 780721 711577

ISBN 978 07217 1157 7
Key Stage 2
Age range 7–11 years
£3.50 (Retail price)